WILLPOWER AND IMPROVE

YOUR MEMORY

TO

THE ULTIMATE

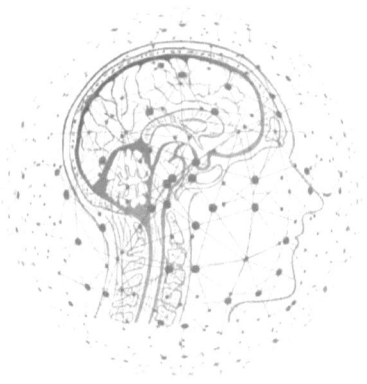

PLEASE VISIT OUR LIBRARY AT

WWW.EBOOKSENGINE.COM

ANDREW MEGAN

Table of Contents

Chapter 1:

It is undeniable that some people tend to be smarter than others. Why this can be hereditary or influenced by specific environments around the growth of an individual; it is also a deliberate action to increase your memory capacity and thus increasing productivity. Some activities, deliberate habits and devotions requesting memory application kick your insight up an indent or two, and the more you draw in your brain along these lines, the more intelligent you most definitely will turn out to be over time.

Analysts undertaking human behavioral studies states that mental practices intended to improve working memory likewise increment scores in "Fluid insight". Fluid insight is the capacity to reason and take care of new issues. It doesn't depend on the mind and is frequently thought of as having a substantial innate segment. Such knowledge is viewed as one of the most significant factors in learning and is connected to scholastic and expert achievement, as indicated by analysts. Discoveries challenge current convictions that the best way to expand fluid insight scores is by legitimately rehearsing on the tests used to figure the score. As of recently, there has been no proof to propose that different sorts of mind preparing would increment such counts in grown-ups.

Just sit back and ask yourself: Suppose I were conceived without a memory. Who might I have been now? Truth is; you surely would be nothing; on the off chance that you don't have a memory, you don't have anything at all. Let's say now I ask you, "Who are you?" you would promptly begin improving recollections in your brain to address that question.

Your memory is the paste that ties your coexistence; all that you are today is a direct result of your beautiful memory. You are an information-gathering being, and your memory is the place your life starts, you wouldn't have the option to learn, think, have and share insights, create things, or even able to wear your clothes; if you had no memory. You wouldn't have the opportunity to construct engagement with any field since experience is only an assortment of recollections all things considered! Just on the off chance that you can recollect data would you be able to live it. However, there is more to only thinking of building up an unlimited memory, and you really wouldn't understand how magnificent and cumbersome your memory capacity is, or even how much you can achieve with just improving on your memory.

We have all had this experience: we perceive and get information, and trying to recall what happened, yet can't review it when we need it. For instance, how many teachers have you met? You obviously must have met so many that you wouldn't remember the exact number, but as the question pops up, you could think of a few.

There is a significant contrast between remembering the number of teachers you've met since you could understand things and resolving the actual number. Did you realize that your quantifiable degree of intelligence level, memory, processing speed, and in general intellectual competence are not for all time set levels?

Also, that, there are things you can do to make yourself a lot more intelligent, regardless of your age?

It's actual, once accepted to be steady past a specific life period, standard science has now acknowledged that we, as a whole, can overhaul our brain from various perspectives.

Chapter 2

What at that point, is the primary strategy for building a superior memory?

When you achieve adulthood, your memory is relied upon to have made an enormous number of neural pathways that naturally helps you with dealing with and audit information quickly, handle fundamental issues and execute continuous assignments within any event mental effort. Nevertheless, on the off chance that you, for the most part, stick to tattered frameworks (Taking a rehashed type of way of life with no adjustment in your day by day schedule), you aren't giving your mind the affectation it needs to keep creating and moving up to improve efficiency. You have to shake things up every so often!

Memory, as solid quality, anticipates that you should "use it or lose it." The more you work out your mind to process things all the more regularly, the better you'll have the alternative to process and remember information quicker and input it all the more viably into creative thoughts. Regardless, not all activities are equal. Notwithstanding, to guarantee satisfactory memory improvement, you have to break your day by day calendar and challenge yourself to use and develop new personality pathways.

It gives you something new. Despite how intellectually mentioning the activity is, if it's something you're starting at now extraordinary at, it is not a better than average personality works out. The development ought to be new and out of your standard scope of commonality. To fortify the psyche, you need to keep learning and developing new capacities.

It isn't really extremely simple. The best personality boosting practices demand your full and close thought. It lacks that you found the activity testing at one point. It ought to at present be something that requires mental effort; for example, attempting to make sense of how to proficiently utilize AutoCAD programming for compositional plans.

So below are a few things to employ to help boost your brainpower and thus improve on your procession speed:

Expand on your Aptitude

Search for exercises that permit you to begin at a single level and stir your way up as your aptitudes improve — continually stretching the limits, so you keep on extending your abilities. At the point when a formerly tedious level begins to feel great, that implies it's an ideal opportunity to handle the following degree of execution.

Treat yourself after reaching a Milestone

Prizes bolster the mind's learning procedure. The more intrigued and connected with you are in the movement, the almost certain you'll keep doing it and the more prominent the advantages you'll encounter. So pick exercises that, while testing, are as yet charming and fulfilling.

There are a significant number of ways contemplation can generally build your memory; intellectual competence, centre, and knowledge.

Handle your health issues in time

Sometimes, we feel our health is taking a massive plunge to the negative, and it is not farfetched. Assuming this is the case, there might be care or lifestyle issue to a fault. It's not merely dementia or Alzheimer's ailment that causes memory misfortune. There are numerous infections, emotional issue, and meds that can meddle with memory. Health Issues like Coronary illnesses, hormonal diseases, Diabetes, hypertension, etc. can affect your memory improvement if not handled in time and accurately and, some cases could lead to protracted disorderliness.

Meditation

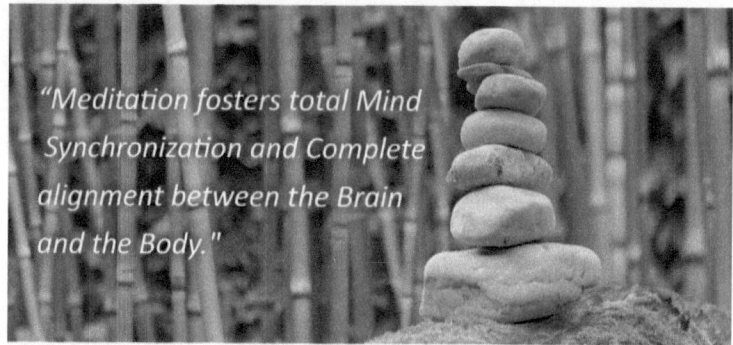

"Meditation fosters total Mind Synchronization and Complete alignment between the Brain and the Body."

Utilizing the most recent in X-ray mind imaging innovation, a milestone 2000 Harvard College study found that in both the short and long haul, reflection specialists regularly and helpfully expanded the neural mass (dark matter) of the cerebrum locales related with long and transient memory, centred consideration, profound idea, and in general intellectual competence while all the while calming the electrical action inside the areas associated with uneasiness, sorrow, dread, and outrage.

As opposed to the generally acknowledged logical assessment of so many decades before now, the neuroplastic nature of our minds implies that our innovative possibilities are not set in hereditary stone — there are sure things we can do to improve its presentation.

Along these lines, much the same as your leg muscles, you can helpfully assemble the quality and even the size of your mind in the most beneficial and generally common of ways. At that point, what is the ideal approach to fabricate a superior memory?

The possibilities of having the option to assemble a superior memory through contemplation are enormous.

Having a super-solid and right mind opens the entryway to a fantastic exhibit of life-changing advantages. To assemble your mind to ever more elevated levels, your sensory system needs an exercise.

Luckily, the neurostimulation from consideration offers your whole tactile framework an uncommonly productive atmosphere, enacting too positive changes all through your body, especially your cerebrum.

In time, your whole tangible framework revises and advances itself on progressively increasingly critical levels, setting up another structure of neural pathways, opening up access between your left and right cerebrum sides of the equator like never before.

This "full personality get to" or "complete personality synchronization," as it's known among setting up scientists, can transform yourself from various perspectives, including boosting your psychological bent, level of knowledge, memory, and understanding.

Science has marginally discovered a trace of something increasingly critical concerning thought's mesmerizing display of memory-boosting benefits.

Eat a brain-boosting diet.
So also, as the body needs fuel, makes the brain. You in all probability understand that

an eating routine reliant on specific items, vegetables, whole grains, "sound" fats, (for instance, olive oil, nuts, fish) and lean protein will give heaps of favourable therapeutic circumstances. However, such an eating routine can, in like manner improve memory. For mind prosperity, in any case, it's not actually what you eat—it's likewise what you don't eat. The going with sustaining tips will help bolster your scholarly ability and decrease your threat of dementia:

Get your omega-3s: Research shows that omega-3 unsaturated fats are particularly valuable for mental prosperity. Fish is a particularly rich wellspring of omega-3, unusually cold water "oily fish, for instance, salmon, fish, halibut, trout, mackerel, sardines, and herring.

If you're not a devotee of fish, consider non-fish wellsprings of omega-3s, for instance, sea development, walnuts, ground flaxseed, flaxseed oil, winter squash, kidney and pinto beans, spinach, broccoli, pumpkin seeds, and soybeans.

Limit calories and inundated fat: Research shows that diets high in immersed fat (from sources, for instance, red meat, entire milk, margarine, cheddar, cream, and solidified yogurt) increase your risk of dementia and incapacitate obsession and memory.

Eat more foods grown from the ground: Produce is loaded down with malignant growth counteraction specialists, substances that shield your neural connections from hurt. Splendid results of the dirt are astoundingly adequate deadly growth counteraction specialist "superfood" sources.

Drink green tea: Green tea contains polyphenols, inconceivable malignant growth counteraction specialists that protected against free radicals that can hurt neurotransmitters. Among various points of interest, balanced usage of green tea may improve memory and mental sharpness and moderate personality developing.

Drink Alcohol with some limitation: Taking alcohol with strict constraint is essential, since alcohol affects the body synapses. Regardless, with some control (around one glass a day for women; 2 for men), alcohol may improve memory and insight. Red wine appears to be the best decision, as it is rich in resveratrol, a flavonoid that lifts the circulatory system as the main priority and reduces the peril of Alzheimer's affliction.

Another eating routine related effect on memory is the mounting research that eating berries can help with warding off memory decline.

An evaluation from the School of Investigating and the Landmass Supportive School found that updating a standard eating routine with blueberries for twelve weeks improved the processing speed of the working memory. The effect of this was seen just a few weeks into the study.

A study on female specialists over the age of 70, found that the people who had by and mainly eaten at any rate two servings of strawberries or blueberries consistently had a moderate diminishing in memory rot. (The effects of strawberries might be asking to be refuted, in any case, since the California Strawberry Commission to some degree upheld that survey and another assessment focusing on strawberries suggested that you'd need to eat around 10 pounds of strawberries for every day to see any effect).

More research is required at this moment; science is moving closer to perceiving how berries may impact our cerebrums. Blueberries are rich in flavonoids, which appear to strengthen the existing relationship as a main priority. That could explain why they're helpful for long stretch memory.

Chapter 3:

Sometimes, do you imagine learning up to ten languages at a stretch or know everything you want to know at will without much stretch of reading for long? Assuming as it were possible, do you know how much more productive you would have been already? Just unfathomable!! The truth is, for a significant number of us, there are a considerable number of things we need to learn than we possess energy for. Furthermore, as data turns out to be all the more promptly available on the web, the number of things we need to learn has just expanded. That implies that the primary variable we can control is the time we spend learning them.

However, there are some things you can employ to enhance your memory speed and thus develop your brain to learn even faster than you could imagine. Here are these few:

Invest at least 30% of your energy in knowing more, and 70% of your time rehearsing:

You can just find out such an enormous amount about how to do an aptitude from examining it. You can invest all the energy you need finding out about how to shoot a soccer ball, yet when you get out there on the pitch, don't hope to have an ideal shot on your first attempt. You comprehend what they state: Careful discipline brings about promising results.

However, in case you're beginning without any preparation, you've found a workable pace look into first; else you won't realize where to start. So what's the correct proportion among training and research? All you need is more practice and learning from the right source.

Try not to rehash an already solved problem:

Why repeat a wheel that is now made? The normal inclination we as a whole have when gaining some new useful knowledge is attempting to ace only it and thinking little of the measure of time and exertion that can be spared by finding support from somebody who's now learned it.

Recall when you originally figured out how to communicate in another dialect or acquire ability. You likely had a precarious expectation to learn and adapt at first, yet following a couple of years or even a very long time of testing and committing errors, you could plan an easy route to enable a companion to evade those equivalent mix-ups you made at a convenient time.

To accomplish authority quicker, our initial step ought to be to counsel the top players in the field and model the way they have just cut out for us. As Robbins puts it: "Numerous incredible pioneers have demonstrated that the quickest method to ace any ability, methodology or objective in life is to display the individuals who have just produced the way forward. If you identify somebody who is as of now getting the outcomes that you need and take similar moves they are making, you can get similar outcomes "It doesn't make a difference what your age, sex or foundation is," Robbins proceeds. "Displaying enables you to fast track your fantasies and accomplish more in a lot shorter timeframe. Right now age, it's conceivable to recover practically any arrangement that is out there as books, websites, preparing recordings, experts, somebody in our system - the rundown goes on."

To cite one more astute individual, this time, Pablo Picasso: "Great specialists duplicate. Incredible specialists take."

Break your skills into parts, and start mastering the most significant parts first:

Deconstructing a task into little pieces doesn't merely cause it to appear to be increasingly sensible; it additionally lets you recognize the most significant things you'll have to learn.

"The vast majority of the things we consider as abilities are in reality large packages of aptitudes that require a wide range of various things," as said by Kaufman in his TED talk. "The more you can break separated the ability, the more you're ready to choose, 'What are the pieces of the aptitude that will assist me with finding a good pace need?'"

At that point, where you can rehearse those things first, it gives you an edge to quickly improve your exhibition in less time. For instance, suppose you need to figure out how to play the violin. You can break that skill down into varied segments like understanding music, stance, appropriate finger placement, learning scales, learning harmonies, fingerpicking, and so on.

So which are the most significant? You may contend that learning natural harmonies and the finger arrangement for those harmonies are two of the most vital abilities, since realizing just a couple of harmonies implies you'll have the option to play a massive amount of tunes.

Deconstruct the skills:

The subsequent stage to hacking the expectation to absorb Information is to deconstruct the ability you see into its essential, necessary parts. Separate the pieces and locate the most significant things to rehearse first.

Incidentally, this idea can apply to nearly anything throughout everyday life, including:

• Business (80 per cent of offers originates from 20 per cent of clients)

• Representative productivity (80 per cent of results originates from 20 per cent of workers)

• Happiness (80 per cent of joy originates from 20 per cent of connections)

• Travel encounters (80 per cent of our movements might be summarized from 20 per cent of our feature encounters)

However, this demonstrates that not very many things have any kind of effect in any part of our lives, including learning. Our objective at that point, ought to be to isolate the 20 per cent of our learning materials that will give us 80 per cent of the outcome.

For no good reason, snappy learning masters have quite recently gotten a handle on this way of thinking, and have given some strong models on the most capable technique to do this satisfactorily. In his TED talk, Josh Kaufman said he accepted that you don't require 10,000 hours to ace an aptitude. Rather, the key is to grasp the first 20 hours and become familiar with the most significant subset abilities inside that time span to get the most excellent measure of effect. Various examinations in the fields of the engine and psychological ability securing have set up that the initial not many long stretches of rehearsing another expertise consistently create the most emotional enhancements in execution.

Quit performing so many tasks at a time:

Performing various tasks is an extravagance we've all created in the period of steady warnings and portable applications. From browsing our messages at regular intervals to looking through our Instagram feed to inviting collaborators stopping by our work area for a "five-minute break": Performing different tasks at a time can be perhaps the most significant obstacle keeping us from adapting quicker.

Take a good look at what happens to your computer or phone when you multitask it, At the point when you have 20 or more various tabs open on your program, your PC starts to back off, and it takes more time to process each activity a while later. Studies have indicated that when an individual gets diverted, it takes a normal of 25 minutes to come back to the job needing to be done. What's progressively essential to note is that an examination by the College of California Irvine found that a specialist puts forth a concentrated effort or herself just 11 minutes before getting occupied.

Something very similar applies to our long haul centre. A considerable lot of us aren't ready to commit the six-to-12, or more months it takes to gain proficiency with expertise in light of the incalculable new activities, thoughts, or diversions that come to our direction. What's more, when we choose to move our concentration to another interruption, it's considerably harder to locate similar energy and drive to concentrate on past expertise.

When you have deconstructed the subset abilities that will give you the most significant measure of results, then, focus exclusively on improving those aptitudes and abstain from picking up whatever else until you've aced them.

Give more time to Adequate Practice:

This is where a large portion of us battle, and what vast numbers of us would prefer not to hear is the standard that acing anything quicker requires practice. Learning requires recurrence of and steadiness in playing out a similar aptitude again and again until you can do it intuitively, without contemplating it.

The best entertainers on the planet comprehend this "mystery" to adapting quicker and become the best, yet once in a while talk about its significance on account of how unsexy it sounds.

Master-level execution is fundamentally the consequence of master level practice, not because of inborn ability, according to K. Anders. Ericsson, a logical scientist from Florida State College, "Individuals accept that since master execution is subjectively not the same as should be expected execution, the master entertainer must be invested with attributes subjectively not quite the same as those of ordinary grown-ups. This view has disheartened researchers from methodically inspecting master entertainers and representing their exhibition as far as the laws and standards of general brain science."

Look for real criticism:

In 1960, while they were as yet an obscure secondary school musical crew, the Beatles went to Hamburg, Germany, to play in the neighborhood clubs. The gathering was come up short on. The acoustics were awful. The crowds were unappreciative.

Then was the take-home lesson from the Hamburg experience for The Beatles? They needed to do more, so they employed relentless long periods of playing time, practice and prompt input that constrained them to improve. That is the crucial distinction that raised the Beatles to the top, as indicated by Malcolm Gladwell in his book Anomalies. The band didn't merely rehearse in a garage for rehearsing sake; they strived to get before a live crowd that would give them prompt analysis and useful criticism.

As the Beatles developed in ability, crowds requested more exhibitions - giving them all the more playing time. By 1962 they were playing eight hours out of each night, seven evenings every week. By 1964, the year they burst on the worldwide scene, the Beatles had played more than 1,200 shows together. By method for correlation, most groups today don't play multiple times in their whole profession.

Apply the 80/20 standard:

It is an idea created by Italian financial analyst Vilfredo Pareto which clarifies that 80% of your ideal yields will originate from just 20% of your sources of info.

While the specific proportion fluctuates from circumstance to circumstance, you'll see that:

Here's your manual for getting unstuck and recovering inspiration!

• 20% of individuals throughout your life will prompt 80% of your   bliss

• 20% of your clients will drive 80% of your deals

• 20% of your learning techniques will prompt 80% of your outcomes

With regards to learning, it feels like there's such a lot of we don't have the foggiest idea, so it's anything but difficult to bounce around all over. This will just prompt sat around idly. What you need to do is the centre around a couple of things that will drive the needle for what you need to accomplish and twofold down on them.

For instance, in case you're learning Spanish to travel this mid-year, rather than figuring out how to compose or peruse, you ought to figure out how to communicate in Spanish. Or on the other hand, as opposed to attempting to satisfy a disappointed client that is just paying you $37/month, you should increase the value of a client that is paying you $1,000/month.

Can't Resist Delaying?

Break down your delaying issue effectively with this free evaluation. You will discover why you've been lingering and how to defeat it.

Chapter 4:

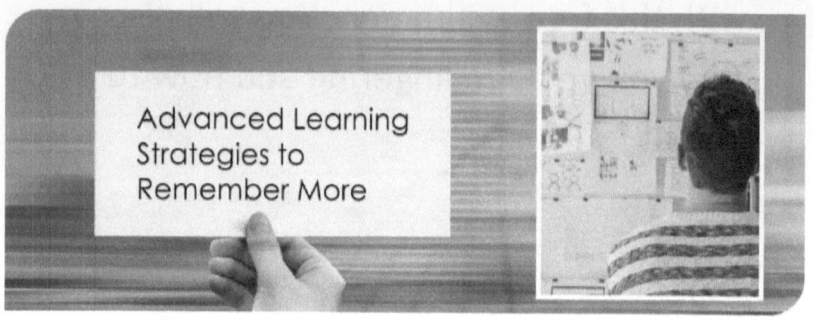

Advanced Learning Strategies to Remember More

State for all to hear what you need to recall. Research shows that contrasted with perusing or thinking quietly (as though there's another method to figure), the demonstration of discourse is a "very amazing component for improving memory for chose data."

As indicated by researchers, "Taking in and memory profit by dynamic contribution. At the point when we include a functioning measure or a creative component to a word, that word turns out to be increasingly particular in long haul memory, and consequently progressively critical."

To put it plainly, while intellectually practicing is acceptable, practicing so anyone can hear is far superior.

Take notes by hand, not on a PC:

The more significant part of us can take notes down quicker than we can compose. Strangely, taking notes by hand improves both cognizance and maintenance, perhaps because rather than merely filling in as a semi stenographer, you're compelled to place things in your own words to keep up.

Which implies you'll recollect what you heard much more.

Perhaps that is the reason Richard Branson has kept up a deep-rooted propensity for keeping a written by hand diary?

Chunk up your examination sessions:

You're occupied. So you hold up until the last moment to realize what you have to know: An introduction, a business demo, a speculator pitch... Research shows "conveyed practice" is a substantially more successful approach to learn.

Envision you need to nail your speculator pitch. When you've drafted your pitch, go through it once. At that point, take a couple of moments to make remedies and amendments.

At that point step away for a couple of hours, or in any event, for a day, before you rehash the procedure.

For what reason does conveyed practice work? The "study-stage recovery hypothesis" says that each time you endeavour to recover something from memory and the recovery is progressively effective, that memory gets more diligently to overlook. (If you go over your pitch more than once, a lot of your introduction is as yet top of the brain... which implies you don't need to recover it from memory.)

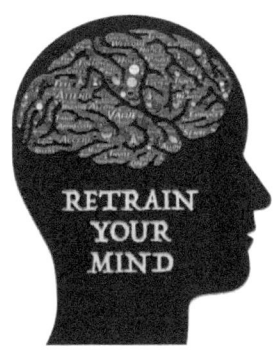

Another hypothesis respects "relevant fluctuation." When data gets encoded into memory, a portion of the setting is additionally encoded. (Which is the reason tuning in to an old tune can make you recollect where you were, what you were feeling, and so on., when you initially heard that tune.) That setting makes helpful signals for recovering data.

Notwithstanding how it functions, disseminated practice unquestionably works. So give yourself sufficient opportunity to scatter your learning sessions. You'll adapt all the more productively and all the more adequately.

Test yourself:
Various evaluations and scientific theory show that self-testing is a very compelling approach to accelerate the learning procedure.

Not entirely that is a result of the additional setting made; in the event that you test yourself and answer erroneously, notwithstanding the way that you will undoubtedly recall the right answer after you discover it... you'll moreover recollect that you didn't review. (Misconception something is a remarkable technique to remember it at whatever point especially if you will, as a rule, be trying for yourself.)

So don't merely rehearse your presentation. Review your capabilities on what you will do after your introduction. Check out yourself by aligning the five most important things you have to do. Endeavour to describe essential bits of knowledge, or arrangements checks, or salary projections...

Not only will you gain trust in the sum you do know, but you'll also even more quickly get acquainted with the things you haven't the faintest idea.

Change how you practice things:

Rehashing anything again and again in the expectations you will ace that errand won't just shield you from improving as fast as possible, now and again it might diminish your expertise.

As indicated by late research from Johns Hopkins, on the off chance that you practice a somewhat changed form of an errand you need to ace, "you find out more and quicker than if you simply continue rehearsing precisely the same thing on numerous occasions in succession." The in all likelihood cause is reconsolidation, a procedure where existing recollections are reviewed and altered with new Information.

Practice the essential skill:

Go through your introduction a few times under similar conditions you'll in the long run face when you do it live. Typically, the second time through will be superior to anything the principal; that is how the practice works.

Know when to halt and restrategize:

Give yourself, in any event, six hours so your memory can combine. (Which most likely methods holding up until tomorrow before you practice once more, which is okay.)

Practice once more, however this time...

Go a little quicker and sometimes slower:

Talk a little - only a few - faster than you ordinarily do. Go through your slides marginally faster. Speeding up implies you'll commit more errors; however, that is alright - simultaneously, you'll change old Information with new Information - and lay the basis for development.

However, something very similar will occur sometimes. (Furthermore, you can try different things with new systems - including the utilization of quiet for impact - that aren't clear when you present at your typical speed.)

Break your introduction into smaller lumps: Pretty much every assignment incorporates a progression of discrete advances. That is certainly valid for introductions. Pick one segment of your presentation. Deconstruct it. Ace it. At that point, put the entire introduction back together.

Change the conditions:

Utilize an alternate projector. Or on the other hand an alternate remote. Or on the other hand a lavaliere rather than a headset mic. Switch up the conditions marginally; not exclusively will that assist you with adjusting a current memory, it will likewise improve you arranged for the unforeseen.

You can stretch out the procedure to nearly anything. While it's unmistakably powerful for learning engine aptitudes, the process can likewise be applied to adapting roughly anything.

Exercise consistently:

Investigation shows that ordinary exercise can improve memory review. Another examination from McMaster College found that times of high-power practice are useful for wellness and memory: Exercise brought about noteworthy upgrades in high-obstruction memory. (Obstruction happens when data that is comparable hinders the data you're attempting to review.)

A generally utilized model for high-obstruction memory is recollecting faces, an expertise that is particularly helpful for individuals planning to make associations.

Exercise additionally brought about an expansion in a substance called BDNF (cerebrum determined neurotrophic factor), a protein that supports the capacity, development, and endurance of synapses.

So: Not exclusively will you feel good on the off chance that you work out, you'll likewise improve your memory.

Get more rest:

Rest is when the more significant part of the memory combination process happens. That is the reason that even a short rest can improve your memory review.

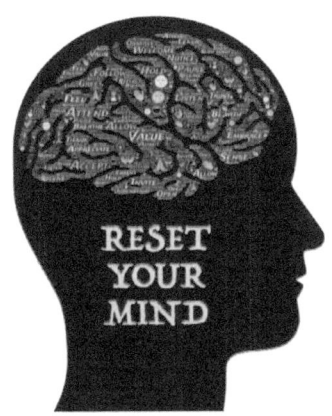

In one investigation members retained delineated cards to test their memory quality. In the wake of remembering a lot of cards, they took a 40-minute break, and one group rested while the other group remained alert. After the break, the two groups were tried on their memory of the cards. The rest bunch performed altogether better, holding by and large 85 per cent of the examples contrasted with 60 per cent for the individuals who had stayed wakeful.

Scientists have additionally discovered that lack of sleep can influence your capacity to submit new data to memory and combine any momentary recollections you have made.

Gain proficiency with a few subjects in progression:

As opposed to blocking (focusing on one issue, one task, or one capacity during a learning session) learn or practice a couple of subjects or aptitudes in movement.

The strategy is called interleaving: Examining related ideas or aptitudes in equal. Also, it turns out interleaving is a considerably more powerful approach to prepare your cerebrum (and your engine aptitudes.)

Why? One hypothesis is that interleaving improves your cerebrum's capacity to separate ideas or abilities. At the point when you square practice one skill, you can penetrate down until muscle memory dominates and the aptitude turns out to be pretty much programmed. At the point when you interleave a few aptitudes, anyone expertise can't get thoughtless - and that is something worth being thankful for. Instead, you're continually compelled to adjust and modify. You're continuously obligated to see, feel, and segregate between various developments or various ideas.

Share the Information you have with other people:

It might be every so often evident that the individuals who can't, instruct... in any case, inquire about shows it's very apparent that the individuals who show accelerate their learning and hold more.

Indeed, even merely believing that you'll have to encourage somebody can cause you to adapt all the more adequately. As per the specialists, "When educators plan to instruct, they will in general search out key focuses and sort out data into a lucid structure. Our outcomes propose that understudies additionally go to these sorts of successful learning procedures when they hope to instruct."

The demonstration of instructing likewise improves Information. Ask any individual who has prepared another person whether they additionally profited by the experience.

Chapter 5:

From multiple points of view, our recollections shape what our identity is. They make up our interior life stories—the narratives we educate ourselves concerning what we've finished with our lives. They disclose to us who we're associated with, who we've contacted during our lives, and who has contacted us. To put it plainly, our recollections are urgent to the embodiment of who we are as people.

That implies age-related memory misfortune can speak to lost self. It likewise influences the handy side of life, such as getting around the area or recalling how to contact a friend or family member. It's not astounding, at that point, that worries about declining thinking and memory aptitudes rank among the top feelings of dread individuals have as they age.

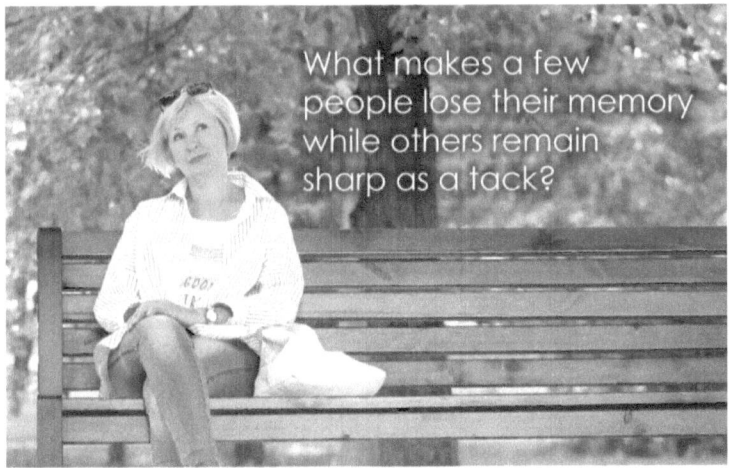

What makes a few people lose their memory while others remain sharp as a tack?

Qualities assume a job, however, do as well decisions. Demonstrated approaches to secure memory incorporate after a sound eating routine, practicing consistently, not smoking, and keeping circulatory strain, cholesterol, and glucose under tight restraints. Carrying on with an intellectually vibrant life is significant, as well. Similarly, as muscles become more grounded with use, mental exercise helps keep mental aptitudes and memory in tone.

Are particular sorts of "mind work" more compelling than others? Any mind practice is superior to being a psychological, habitually, lazy person. In any case, the exercises with the most effective are those that expect you to work past what is agreeable and straightforward. Playing unlimited rounds of solitaire and viewing the most recent narrative long-distance race on the History Channel may not be sufficient. Learning another dialect, volunteering, and different exercises that strain your cerebrum are better wagers.

Look over a couple of techniques to help recall the names of individuals you meet, yet there are parcels to state about memory.

For no good reason, science is continually finding new relationships between direct things we can venture into daily, and enhance our unlimited memory. Memory is a jumbled method that is involved in several different cerebra works out.

Making A Memory

Our psyche bestows signs in a particular model identified with the event we're experiencing and makes the relationship between our neurons, called synapses.

Reviewing The Memory

In case we didn't do anything further, that memory would fall legitimately out of our heads again. An association is a route toward submitting it too long stretch memory so we can audit it later. A vast amount of this technique happens while we're resting, as our personalities repeat that equal case of cerebrum development to strengthen the neural associations we made previously.

Exploring The Memory

This is what most of us consider when we talk about memory, or especially memory incident. Exploring the memory is increasingly direct if it's been fortified after some time, and each time we do in that capacity, we experience that equal case of mind development again, making it to some degree more grounded.

Memory adversity is a fair bit of developing, yet that doesn't mean we can't make a transition to back it off a piece. We ought to examine a part of the habits wherein inquire about has found to keep our memories around to the degree this would be conceivable.

Think To Improve Your Memory Limit

Memory Limit, which is to some degree like the mind's scratchpad, is the spot new information is held quickly. Right when you gain capability with someone's name or hear the area of a spot you're going to, you hold tight to those nuances in working memory until you're done with them. In the occasion that they're not helping any more, you let go of them. In case they are, you submit them to long stretch memory where they can be strengthened and looked into later.

Research has demonstrated that individuals with no association with careful examination can improve their memory audit in just two months. Reflection, with its ability to empower us to centre, has moreover been seemed to improve state-managed test scores and working memory limits after only two weeks.

For what reason does thought advantage memory? It's, somewhat, nonsensical.

During reflection, our cerebrums quit taking care of information as viably as they conventionally would.

In the image underneath you can see how the beta waves (showed up in beautiful tones on the left), which exhibit that our psyches are taking care of information, are substantially diminished during thought (on the right).

Drink Coffee To Improve Your Memory Strength

Whether or not caffeine can improve memory at whatever point taken before increasing some new helpful information is a long way from being correct. Most research has found no effect from ingesting caffeine before making new memories.

One progressive test, regardless, found that taking a caffeine pill after learning greatly enhanced memory retention ability by 24 hours. A selected number of people were made to recollect pictures and then asked to overview similar pictures (targets), practically identical pictures (draws) and different pictures (foils). The point was to pick what pictures they unequivocally recalled, without being misled by the draws which were generally equivalent to. This is a methodology called plan separation, which, as shown by the experts, reflects an "increasingly significant level of memory upkeep."

The examiners right now on the effects of caffeine on memory association: the path toward strengthening the memories we've made. This is they acknowledge there were impacts when caffeine because ingested after the learning task, instead of beforehand.

Exercise To Improve Your Memory

Amasses in both rat and human personalities have demonstrated that conventional exercise can improve memory audit. Wellbeing in progressively prepared adults has even been shown to slow the decline of memory without the guide of continued with regular exercise.

In particular, examines exhibited that customary exercise can improve spatial memory, so it is anything but a way to deal with upgrade a broad scope of memory audit.

The upsides of every action fluctuate, yet for the brain explicitly, solid exercise seems to improve theoretical limits memory. Thus if you're reviewing ways to deal with stay sharp mentally, taking a walk could be the proper reaction. See how an energetic walk ignites the brain in the yield underneath:

Eat Gums to expand your cerebra processing speed

Another straightforward procedure to endeavour that could improve your memory is gnawing gum while you embrace new things. There's been some contradicting investigation around this subject, so it is not a significant bet. In any case, an examination dispersed a year prior showed that individuals who completed a memory audit task were progressively definite and had higher reaction times if they bit gum during the assessment.

One clarification that gnawing gum may impact our memory survey is that it grows development in the hippocampus, a large part of the brain for memory. It's up 'til now foggy why this happens, be that as it may.

Another speculation revolves around the extension of oxygen from just chewing gum, which can help with focus and thought. This could mean we're making a more grounded relationship in the cerebrum as we adjust new things while biting gum. One examination found that individuals who chewed gum during learning and memory tests had higher heartbeat levels than control social affairs, which can, in like manner, brief more oxygen spilling to the cerebrum.

Chapter 6

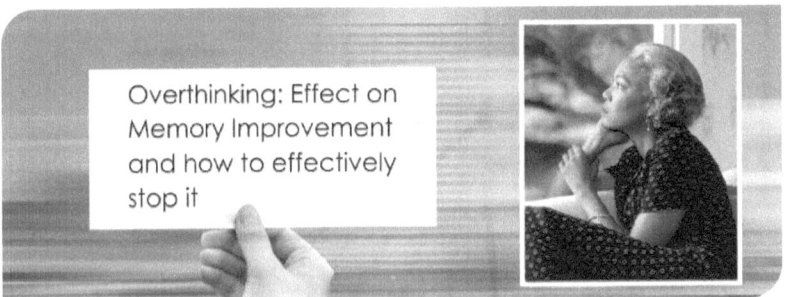

Overthinking: Effect on Memory Improvement and how to effectively stop it

The truth that most people do not understand how far overthinking affects their memory power and unlimited capacity of their brain. Let's you lost in a straightforward competition, and you feel down for a while, somehow it is natural to feel so.

But what is harmful is when you allow this process to stay longer than usual. In any case, when you run that pitiful situation again and again in your mind, it will undoubtedly shape undesirable associations in your brain, and the outcome can be extremely troubling.

This sort of rumination is called "overthinking" in lay terms, and keeping in mind that we as a whole are liable of it somewhat, however, Serious overthinking is terrible for your mental wellbeing.

Overthinking is a well-known human daily life issue, and sometimes it can happen as a result of stress. Stress occurs regularly, and it comes in different forms; the pressure of attempting to shuffle family, work, and school duties together. It may include issues like lifestyle, cash, and connections. In each case where we face potential danger, our psyches and bodies go vigorously, preparing to either manage the issues or entirely stay away from the problem.

You have most likely heard about how awful pressure is for your brain and body. It can prompt physical manifestations, for example, cerebral pains and chest torment. It can deliver mindset issues, for example, nervousness or misery. It can even provoke social issues, for instance, upheavals of outrage or indulging.

What you cannot deny is that pressure can likewise seriously affect your mind. Despite the stress, your mind experiences a progression of responses – some great and some terrible—intended to assemble and shield itself from potential dangers. Some of the time, pressure can help hone the mind and improve the capacity to recall insights regarding what's going on.

Impact of Overthinking on Memory Improvement

As cited earlier, if Overthinking is allowed for a long time, it could be detrimental to the mind and the general well being of the human memory. However, below are a few possible impacts on memory improvement

Memory Issues

Stress can likewise influence your memory and your enthusiastic capacities. Being unpleasant can expand your odds of memory misfortune. Moreover, stress can also make you progressively excited. A distressing individual partner's sensible undertakings with the feeling which winds up trading off their decisions.

Dread And Uneasiness

Overthinking can expand the exercises in the amygdala (Dread Focus of the brain tissues). You become increasingly dreadful and pushed. Which consequently makes more pressure start with.

Inhibited Synapses

Our body is continually developing. Each bone, each muscle, each cell is being devastated and being created continuously. Yet, overthinking can slow the procedure of recovery of synapses.

Very Prone to Psychological issues

Overthinking can likewise cause physical and social changes. It can also build the odds of dysfunctional behaviour. Nervousness, alarm issue, melancholy, PTSD, bipolar issue, fixation, and liquor abuse are a portion of the problems an individual can confront.

Getting Inept

Recall that feeling when you are too anxious even to consider saying anything (Particularly in interviews), also though you know the appropriate response. This is typically happening a direct result of pressure and overthinking. Severe pressure can drain your essential leadership, subjective capacities, and critical thinking aptitudes.

How to Quit Overthinking and Enhance Unlimited Memory

Overthinking can be avoided or stopped even when it is has become a usual process. It isn't a mission impossible, and anyone can easily cub this issue by applying this few steps:

Catch yourself: This is the hardest part because more often than not, we don't understand that we are overthinking. Along these lines, work on scrutinizing your negative contemplations consistently.

An attribute of overthinking is they are frequently summed up or obscure, similar to "I realize I will bomb the test" or "Consider the possibility that I can't wake up on schedule. Perceive this tone of your idea and stop yourself. Reflection and care strategies are an extraordinary method to improve this capacity.

Allow it to out: The more you keep these considerations inside you, the more they will influence. Figure out how to allow them to out. Record them by point, or verbalize them by conversing with somebody close and trusted. At the point when you compose or let them know, you are giving them a reasonable verbalization, and are better set to confront it. Frequently, during the time spent composition or telling, we understand the contrasts to the negative considerations without anyone else's input.

Get going: Perhaps the surest approaches to quit overthinking are to redirect your brain on some other errand. When you find yourself overthinking, promptly and intentionally take up some work that is irrelevant to your considerations. You can deal with an alternate task, practice craftsmanship, or enjoy any side interest you like. Exercise is additionally an extraordinary method to clear up an exhausted cerebrum, as it has a few different advantages as well.

Put your time in a safe spot: Put an alert on your rumination time. Put aside 10-15 minutes (not very long a period) every day to consider everything. When that time is past and the caution rings, mightily take your psyche somewhere else. This will stop the negative idea circuits from flourishing in your memory, and after some time, these will blur and quit influencing your prosperity.

Look for help: Overthinking is related to depression and sentiment of not being comprehended. Whenever you feel you are overthinking, talk about it to somebody you can trust, or look for the help of an expert advisor.

Chapter 7:

Become More
Productive

You can't hope to be increasingly more resourceful and productive by nor investing time to build your memory to a comfortable piece. You most likely would go through hard days of developing your work propensities both great and terrible, deliberately or intuitively and those won't promptly change.

Little alterations can inspire all the more enduring changes, yet those may require some serious energy and order. It looks incredibly straightforward when you're scrutinizing an effectiveness article like this to trust it's necessary. Nevertheless, it's most certainly not. I'm not making this from a pro viewpoint, yet from related work in the fight against interference.

Notwithstanding, turning out to be progressively beneficial is a purposeful activity, and no one but you can choose to be increasingly gainful all alone. Numerous individuals just wish they could utilize more bit of their memory capacity to work, to be more productive than they used to be; however, they would prefer not to give in their best to oversee that come. Thus, on the off chance that you will turn out to be increasingly profitable throughout everyday life, at that point, you would need to apply this couple of purposeful strides throughout your life.

Make a reasonable arrangement for the afternoon:

Do whatever it takes not to overwhelm yourself. Plan for the day often crashes and burns since we make them too much astounding or the assignments are conflicting. A couple of tasks will take a long time; others won't take at whatever point in any way, shape or form. This makes an unbalanced state, in the way we pass on and utilize our time. What happens then is that our arrangement the day by then transforms into a postponing instrument. The fact of the matter is out. From that point forward, we do the basic stuff, and a short time later, become involved in the hard thing.

Mind Mapping:
Mind Maps (similarly called thought maps or memory maps) are a convincing strategy

to interface contemplations and thoughts in your cerebrum, and a short time later "see" the affiliations firsthand. Mind Mapping is a note-taking system that records information to such an extent that gives you how various bits of information fit together. There's truth in the adage "A picture talks a thousand words", and mind maps make a successfully reviewed "picture" of the information you're endeavoring to remember.

This technique is significant to diagram and solidify information from an arrangement of sources. It, in like manner, allows you to think about complex issues in the same way, and a short time later present your revelation with the end goal that shows the nuances similarly as the 10,000-foot see.

Set short term goals for each task:

With each new endeavour or errand, the expansion may give off an impression of being too much gigantic. Regardless, when you start isolating it and recognizing what can be rehearsed, you'll notice how each part develops the other.

One of the most direct and most sensible things you can do is to isolate your advancing endeavour or deliverable into more diminutive destinations. What are the pieces and assets required? Who do you need to chat with first? Separate these pieces before setting courses of occasions, and a while later check to what degree they'll take you to accomplish.

Understanding the degree of what's being asked, setting up the methods and a while later evaluating the time required will help you with taking a few to get back some composure of what's being asked.

Identify what steals most of your time:

We all in all have time punks, yet a large segment of us have no idea what they are. If you can recognize your most prominent time lawbreakers, the activities or conditions that lose you a course, possess or encroach upon you, or the awful affinities that shield you from performing better, you will improve your results generously more quickly.

On the off chance that you endeavour to consider and apply different strategies, and you disregard your present hooligans, the effort will remain trivial.

If you plan to change one of your most discernibly horrible time the load up affinities, you will improve your results immediately. It will no uncertainty moreover give you the power to change what else isn't working when you feel the prize of your undertakings, and you see the apparent relationship between what you do and what your reality is.

Consider certain things which in case you changed as of now, would have the most noteworthy beneficial outcome on your productivity. Record this, consider what causes or adds to this and what your answer will push ahead.

Identify your Best time of Maximum Functionality:

A couple of us are morning people; a couple of us are night owls. In any case, the propelled business condition doesn't agree with the nightlife. Maybe the work environment doesn't open until 9, yet your zenith is from 5 am to 7 am. Before long, it is found that there are high essentialness levels when a considerable number of individuals are loosening up their day, around 4 pm to 7 pm and a while later after 8 pm. Now, what you have to do is simply purposely delegate some time or timetable even more less-key assignments during hours when you are not as connected. It's suggested that we ought to find at any pace of 2 hours consistently to bounce into the harder basic work and leave many hours for social events or less sincere assignments.

You'll also recognize structures and when you could participate in "significant work" or focused work for longer time allotments. This is the thought from Georgetown teacher Cal Newport. Some work (like taking note of messages) is shallow, while others (like considering new campaign thoughts or remarkable photo modifying)

may require progressively connected with
time or "significant work."

Pick one task and another after that:

This is very serious, considering the way
that every so often our endeavours aren't a
30-minute or one hour work. It may take 8
hours or many days. What's the proper
reaction by then? Split it up into one task
and a short time later do that one

endeavour to its summit. In any case, to what degree should that be?

Besides, what's reasonable? I contemplate our days are broken into four segments. Which by then is incredibly 45 to 50 minutes. We have get-togethers that start on the hour, or we take a mid-day break, or we plan a require an hour. Working dependably for 45 minutes on one thing looks good, be that as it may, is problematic.

The Pomodoro method proposes brief squares of time, with short, concise breaks, trailed by longer breaks later on.

Pomodoro urges you to clear out impedances and makes you measure to what degree a particular task will take you. Examine progressively about the Pomodoro system at present.

Dispose of some unwanted stuffs and Declutter at some point:

Did you understand your physical condition impacts your work? Likewise, I don't mean just in case you work in a "cool" office or not. Dependent upon your association and your activity in the association that is out of your control. Nevertheless, you can control your workspace. It causes you to be logically beneficial when you don't have to pursue and peck for whatever that missing thing is. It causes you to be progressively profitable when you don't need to chase and bite for whatever that missing thing is. You'll spare time by not doing that. You'll likewise get greater clarity and centre for your jobs needing to be done.

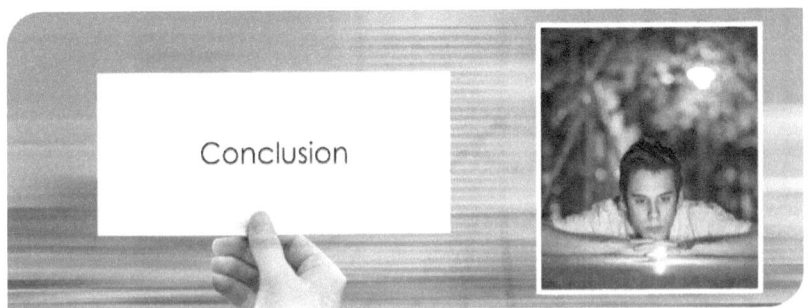

Conclusion

For what reason would you like to improve your memory?

Is it true that you are searching for an edge in school, to contend, have some slick stunts at parties? There are very many reasons why many people want an unlimited memory or most importantly want to upgrade their memory.

You might stumble few reasons as you surf the web and look for solutions, but what is eminent is that people are utilizing memory upgrade in a way that recommends that their inspiration is something other than for just fun.

An unlimited memory is an edge you need at work, school and generally in life, to live that superhero life you so desire. You could generally be savvy enough to make do with crude ability.

However, this book will help you utilize your unlimited memory to recall things better faster and make quicker progressive decisions for your life. How would you feel like a student, to quickly and effortlessly bind your physiology notes to the strategy for loci? Feels great, right? And you can so rapidly build on your test scores even at short notice.

Many marriages are torn apart because partners quickly forget things that matter to their spouses, they could easily overlook birthday events, forget important things they've learnt, or even forget arrangements.

Having perused around the subject a great deal, I genuinely feel I have gone 'down the hare opening' - what can be accomplished has far outperformed my most out of this world fantasies. These above-listed approaches would help you improve your memory and unlock your unlimited memory. You just don't know how amazing you are underneath the skin; you can do more than you think.

Thank you for reading..

Please put your review of the book,